Table of contents

Executive summary

When a debt is seriously delinquent and the creditor sells the debt or refers the debt either to a collection agency or to an internal collection department, the collector or creditor can separately report the account to one or more of the three largest nationwide consumer reporting agencies (NCRAs) as an account in collections. The presence of a collections tradeline can have a negative impact on a consumer's credit score. [1]

There are currently an estimated 220 million consumers with a credit report at one or more of the NCRAs.[2] Collections tradelines affect the reports of nearly one out of three of these consumers. Consumers are far more likely to dispute the accuracy of these tradelines than of other information contained on their credit reports.

Roughly half of all collections tradelines that appear on credit reports are reported by debt collectors seeking to collect on medical bills claimed to be owed to hospitals and other medical providers. These medical debt collections tradelines affect the credit reports of nearly one-fifth of all consumers in the credit reporting system.

This paper describes characteristics of the medical and non-medical collections tradelines on consumers' credit reports and the processes by which they appear and disappear. It draws on analysis of data contained in the Consumer Financial Protection Bureau's (CFPB) Consumer

---

[1] 'Tradeline' is defined as an entry by a credit grantor to a consumer's credit history maintained by a credit reporting agency. A tradeline describes the consumer's account status and activity. Tradeline information includes names of companies where the applicant has accounts, dates accounts were opened, credit limits, types of accounts, balances owed and payment histories. In this report, "tradeline" refers to both active accounts and accounts designated as collections. http://www.experian.com/credit-education/glossary.html.

[2] Frequently Asked Questions on Credit Reports, Experian (Nov 25, 2014), http://www.experian.com/ourcommitment/credit-report-faqs.html.

Page Left Blank

Credit Panel (CCP); consumer complaints to the CFPB about collections; and interviews with debt collection agencies, healthcare providers, and other observers of the healthcare billing and payment processes. The CFPB has not sought to verify original research introduced in this paper through its supervisory authorities. The paper does not draw upon supervisory information the CFPB has learned through examinations it has conducted, and does not make conclusions about whether any specific market participants are in compliance with particular statutes or rules pertaining to consumer reporting.

Key findings

Collections tradelines affect many consumers. Nearly one-third of consumers with credit reports (31.6 percent) have one or more collections tradelines on their credit reports. About 19.5 percent of credit reports - nearly one in five - contain one or more medical collections tradelines, while 24.5 percent contain one or more non-medical tradelines.

Most collections tradelines result from unpaid bills rather than unpaid loans. Over half are medical.

More than two-thirds of all collections tradelines (67.5 percent) – and over 80 percent of those tradelines that can be attributed to a particular creditor or provider -- are reported on accounts that originated with a healthcare provider, utility company, or telecommunications company. These are companies that generally do not regularly report payment history to the NCRAs and almost all rely on their collection agencies to report on accounts in collections. Medical collections tradelines account for over half (52.1 percent) of all collections tradelines with an identifiable creditor or provider.

Most collections tradelines are for small amounts. Medical collections tradelines are even smaller than non-medical tradelines. The median unpaid non-medical collections tradeline is $366 (with an average of $1,000). Medical unpaid collections tradelines are even smaller with a median of $207 and average of $579. These contrast with the much larger amounts that are due on credit cards or student loans that are seriously delinquent (more than 120 or 150 days past due). Such accounts average several thousand dollars.

Information on collections tradelines are furnished to the three largest nationwide consumer reporting agencies by a vast array of collectors. We can identify approximately 1,400 different entities that furnish collections account information in our 5 percent sample of credit reports. The degree of fragmentation varies significantly by the type of debt in collections. Medical debt reporting is highly fragmented, with the top furnisher accounting for only 3 percent of medical collections tradelines and the top 10 furnishers accounting for only 18 percent of those tradelines. In contrast, the top furnisher for telecommunications collections accounts for 37 percent of collections tradelines while the top 10 furnishers account for 83 percent of collections tradelines in that industry.

Third-party contingency collectors who furnish much of the collections tradeline information have indirect and short term ties to the underlying debt. Third-party collectors report information about their accounts in collections only during the time that they are assigned the accounts by their creditor clients. Most of these tradelines appear on credit reports when the account is assigned to the third party, and then disappear or "fall-off"the report at the end of the assignment period. Rates of fall-off vary by collections type, with medical debt having a lower fall-off rate than other types of collections tradelines. The large number of collectors furnishing information on collections tradelines and their indirect affiliation with the debt introduces potential sources of error in collections reporting.

Collections tradelines can represent a wide variety of consumer circumstances when they appear on credit reports. There are no objective or enforceable standards that determine when a debt can or should be reported as a collections tradeline. Creditors may elect to sell a debt to a debt buyer or send a debt to a third-party collections agency or in-house collections department at varying times in the collection cycle. Debt buyers and collectors determine whether, when, and for how long to report a collections account as a collections tradeline. Practices vary by type of account and within particular industries. Because of these variations, there is only a limited relationship between the recency and severity or of a delinquency and when or whether a collections tradeline appears on a consumer's credit report.

Medical bills can be a cause of confusion and uncertainty and can result in collections tradelines for consumers who are uncertain about what they owe, to whom, when, or for what. The process of incurring medical expenses and the process by which such expenses are turned into medical bills differs from recurring bills issued by installment lenders, credit card companies, utilities, and telecommunications companies. Lack of price transparency and the complex system of insurance coverage and cost sharing means many consumers, including those who have health coverage, receive medical bills that are a source of confusion. Among consumers who have submitted complaints to the Bureau about debt collection problems, medical collections complaints are much more likely to be about the existence, amount, or information pertaining to the debt than non-medical collections complaints.

A large portion of consumers with medical debts in collections show no other evidence of financial distress and are consumers who ordinarily pay their other financial obligations on time. 22 percent of consumers with collections tradelines (7 percent of all consumers with credit reports) have only medical collections tradelines. These consumers owe less, have more available credit which they could use to repay their debt, and are more reliable payers than consumers with non-medical collections tradelines or than consumers with both types of collections tradelines. Indeed, of the consumers with only medical collections tradelines, approximately 50 percent have otherwise "clean" credit reports with no indication of serious past delinquencies.

Recently proposed rules and recently issued industry best practices pertaining to medical billing and collections practices may help standardize the timing of when collectors furnish information about medical debts in collections to the NCRAs. These developments could reduce the number of medical collections tradelines that appear on consumers' records in situations in which the consumer is uncertain about what she/he owes, to whom, and for what. These developments may also promise greater robustness in the way that credit scores can interpret the presence of a medical collection tradeline on a credit report.

The Bureau will continue its efforts to assess the accuracy of information reported to and contained on credit reports and to identify steps that various stakeholders can take to improve the accuracy, integrity, and consistency of data in the system, consumers' awareness of how the system works, and consumers' ability to make sure their credit reports accurately represent their credit histories.

1. Introduction—the reporting of collections tradelines

1.1 Collections tradelines: a signal of financial distress and impact on credit scores

When a consumer falls behind on payments of a loan or other bill, the entity owed will ordinarily make efforts to collect the amount due. During the early stages of delinquency, the effort may consist of no more than a reminder notice or call about the outstanding obligation. As the length of delinquency increases, so can the intensity of the collection activity. Eventually, the creditor can refer the account to an in-house collections department, assign it to a third-party debt collector, or sell the account to a debt buyer. Once the account is in collections, the creditor, debt collector, or debt buyer can report the account to one or more of the three largest nationwide consumer reporting agencies (NCRAs).[3] When this occurs, the account will appear on the consumer's credit report as an "account in collection," referred to as a "collections tradeline" in this paper.

Generally, the credit industry interprets the presence of a collections tradeline above a certain minimum amount on a consumer's credit report as a signal that the consumer is experiencing

---

[3] These companies (TransUnion, Equifax, and Experian) are described in the Consumer Financial Protection Bureau's December 2012 white paper. *See* Consumer Financial Protection Bureau, Key Dimensions and Processes in the U.S. Credit Reporting System: A review of how the nation's largest credit bureaus manage consumer data (September 2012) *available at* http://files.consumerfinance.gov/f/201212_cfpb_credit-reporting-white-paper.pdf.

difficulty or reluctance in meeting his or her financial obligations. When present, a collections tradeline is incorporated as a derogatory factor in most credit scoring models, which use credit report information to predict a consumer's likelihood of repaying debts. For example, the Fair Isaac Corporation (FICO) reports that for one of its recent scoring models (FICO 8), the addition of any paid or unpaid collections tradeline of at least $100 to a consumer's credit report will reduce a score of 680 by over 40 points and a score of 780 by over 100 points.[4,5] Such a significant drop in a credit score will generally increase a consumer's cost of borrowing credit and in some instances will preclude him or her from accessing the credit market.

In the Bureau's representative sample of consumer credit reports, 9.1 percent of all tradelines reported on consumer credit reports as of December 2012 were labeled as collections tradelines.[6, 7]

---

[4] FICO develops and licenses the most widely used scoring models (although many other score models are used by lenders), which typically generate scores ranging between 300 and 850 points. Other score developers also license scoring models for use by lenders. For more information about the credit scoring market and scores used by lenders, see Consumer Financial Protection Bureau, Analysis of Differences between Consumer- and Creditor-Purchased Credit Scores at 3-4 (September 2012) *available at* http://files.consumerfinance.gov/f/201209_Analysis_Differences_Consumer_Credit.pdf.

[5] Letter from Fair Isaac Corporation (FICO), to authors (Oct.21, 2014) (on file with CFPB).

[6] Data on the incidence and characteristics of collections tradelines on credit reports used in this study come from the CFPB's CCP. The CCP is a longitudinal, nationally representative sample of approximately 5 million de-identified credit records from one of the NCRAs. The sample provides tradeline-level information for all of the tradelines associated with each credit report or record each month, including collections debts of these consumers; the record also includes a commercially-available credit score. The record-level information that is included in the sample allows us to identify which debts reported by third-party collection agencies were from medical or non-medical debts. While we can identify those collections that were from medical debt, nothing in the data reveals information about the identity of the medical service provider(or consumer), the type of institution that provided the service, or the nature of the services that were performed.

We analyze data from the CCP in two timeframes:

The first dataset depicts a snapshot of all consumer credit reports in the panel as of December 2012 for a random sample of 4.95 million consumers and their corresponding 76.8 million tradelines. This dataset provides insight into the incidence of collections tradelines, how frequently they appear on credit reports, and statistics on the sizes and types of collections tradelines.

The second dataset is a time series depiction of approximately 234,000 collections tradelines that their respective furnishers first reported on consumer reporting agency in January of 2013. (These tradelines may have been

Not all accounts that become seriously delinquent end up being reported to the NCRAs as collections tradelines. Some creditors simply choose not to furnish information about their accounts, as the U.S. credit reporting system is a voluntary system. For entities that do opt to furnish, NCRA guidelines define ways in which delinquencies can be designated.[8] Frequently, for example, lenders who regularly furnish information about their borrowers' accounts can update the payment status information about an account to indicate that the payment is 30, 60, 90, 120 days (etc.) or more delinquent. The furnisher can also add a code indicating that it has recognized a charge-off on the loan or debt. [9,10] Our research indicates that most credit card issuers and student loan servicers furnish information about their seriously delinquent accounts to the NCRAs using days delinquent to denote the severity of the delinquency. While the credit card issuers and student loan servicers are likely to have assigned such accounts to a collection agency or to an internal collections department of the creditor, these accounts do not appear as separately designated collections tradelines on credit reports.

Among the 90.9 percent of accounts that were reported as active tradelines as of December 31, 2012, 2.1 percent of tradelines were at least 150 days past due and 3.6 percent of tradelines were at least 120 days past due. A credit risk manager or credit scoring model can interpret an active tradeline that appears this severely delinquent in similar ways to how they interpret a collections

---

recently been referred to a debt collector, or they may have been re-assigned by the creditor from one collector to another or sold to a debt buyer. In the latter cases, the account may previously have appeared as a collections tradeline furnished by another collector. The time series tracks these tradelines as first reported by furnishers and then as they continue to appear on (or disappear from) credit reports in each of the subsequent months ending in June, 2014. This sample provides visibility into the lifecycle of collections tradelines as they are reported by individual furnishers. Because the panel does not identify original creditors associated with accounts in collections, we are unable to easily track how these same collections tradelines were reported after they are reassigned from one debt collector to another or sold by an original creditor to a debt buyer.

[7] Under industry reporting guidelines, a "Collections Account" is described as "Account seriously past due/account assigned to attorney, debt collection agency, or credit grantor's internal collections department."

[8] The Consumer Data Industry Association (CDIA) provides guidance to debt collection agencies through its "Metro 2®" guidelines for furnishers to the NCRAs.

[9] Charge-off is defined for the purposes of this report as a debt that is deemed uncollectible by the credit provider and is subsequently written off. This type will be classified as 'bad debt expense' on the income statement, and removed from the balance sheet.

[10] We use the terms "furnish" and "furnisher" to refer respectively to the act of reporting consumer information to one of these companies and to any entity that reports such information.

tradeline: both are viewed as signals that the consumer can have serious difficulty and/or can lack motivation in meeting his or her financial obligations.

Once an active account is closed, NCRA guidelines provide an alternative means by which the account can be reflected on a credit report. At that point, the guidelines permit the account to be reported as a collections tradeline. In addition, entities that do not regularly furnish information on the status of their accounts – for example, utility companies or telecommunications companies – can report a collections tradeline to the NCRAs after they have referred their accounts to collections. [11] Debt collection agencies – when permitted or instructed by the creditor – and debt buyers may also furnish information to the NCRAs about accounts on which they are seeking to collect. When they do, the only reporting option permitted under the NCRA guidelines is to report the accounts as collections tradelines.

This paper focuses on the account information that is furnished distinctly as collections tradelines. While industry guidelines permit these accounts to be furnished by either creditors or collectors, in practice, the vast majority of collections tradelines are furnished by third-party debt collectors or debt buyers.[12]

In our December 2012 snapshot of consumer credit report information, approximately 8.4 percent of collections tradelines appearing on credit reports are reported as paid in full or settled for an amount less than the full balance. When a collections tradeline is recognized as paid, the balance reported as owed is changed from an outstanding amount to zero.[13] Until recently, most credit scoring models have recognized both paid collections tradelines and unpaid collections tradelines above a certain minimal amount as indicators of financial difficulty or unwillingness to pay on the part of the consumer.

---

[11] A closed account may include indicators as to the reason for closure. Specific codes may indicate that an account was discharged in bankruptcy, that it was sold to a debt buyer, or that it was paid and closed by the consumer. When a furnisher reports an account as closed, it is not deleting the account (deletion is discussed later in this paper). When an account is reported as closed, the associated tradeline may continue to appear on a credit report as a closed account. In contrast, when a furnisher deletes a tradeline, information about the account will no longer appear on the consumer's credit report.

[12] Industry interviews indicate that a small portion of collections tradelines are furnished by the original creditor, however, we are unable to precisely quantify this share of all tradelines from the indicators contained in our sample of credit report information.

[13] According to Metro 2® guidelines, paid in full and settled accounts should not be deleted.

Both unpaid and paid collections tradelines also represent derogatory information that is subject to restrictions under the Fair Credit Reporting Act (FCRA) as to how long from the date of the original delinquency the item is permitted to appear on most credit reports (seven years for most debts and ten years for bankruptcies, after which the item must be omitted from the report).[14]

In our sample, 82.5 percent of the collections tradelines appear with an indicator designating the industry from which the debt originated (17.5% were missing the industry designation). Approximately two thirds (67.5 percent) of collections tradelines consist of debts owed to utilities, telephone, wireless, and cable companies and amounts owed on medical bills. [15] Medical bills comprise approximately half of all collections tradelines.

1.2 Concerns about furnishing practices of debt collectors

In the course of its market monitoring, supervisory, and consumer response activity, the CFPB has sought to learn more about the accuracy, integrity, and consistency of information reported to the NCRAs. Information from recent studies of credit report accuracy and from other sources

---

[14] As per the Fair Credit Reporting Act, information excluded from credit reports include accounts placed for collection or charged to profit and loss which antedate the report by more than seven years. The seven year period "[...] shall begin, with respect to any delinquent account that is placed for collection (internally or by referral to a third party, whichever is earlier), charged to profit and loss, or subjected to any similar action, upon the expiration of the 180-day period beginning on the date of the commencement of the delinquency which immediately preceded the collection activity, charge to profit and loss, or similar action." Exemptions to these time limits are found in 15U.S.C. §1681c (2012).

[15] This statistic factors in the 17.5 percent of collections tradelines for which an original creditor classification may be missing. If we excluded these unclassified items from the sample, the collections tradelines that originated with a medical provider or with a utility, telephone, wireless, or cable company would represent 81.8 percent of all collections tradelines in our sample.

raise particular concerns about the accuracy and interpretation of collections tradelines, the vast majority of which are furnished by debt collection agencies and debt buyers.[16,17,18]

- In its 2012 white paper on the U.S. credit reporting system, the CFPB reported (based on interviews with the three largest NCRAs) that debts in collections accounted for 13 percent of tradelines in credit reports.[19] These tradelines however, accounted for nearly 40 percent of consumer disputes about inaccurate information handled by the NCRAs through e-OSCAR, the online dispute system used by data furnishers and the NCRAs to create and respond to consumer credit history disputes. [20]

---

[16] The Federal Trade Commission (FTC) found that 5 percent of consumer records had errors that could negatively impact a consumer's ability to get favorable loan terms. The study observed that one in four consumers (24 percent) identified what they believed to be an error on at least one of their three credit reports from an NCRA. Among 1,001 consumers who reviewed their credit reports, collections tradelines accounted for 502 of 1,210 alleged inaccuracies identified by consumers regarding non-header information on their credit reports. Collections tradelines accounted for 267 of 662 errors that were modified following consumer disputes regarding non-header information.

[17] Federal Trade Commission, Report to Congress under Section 319 of the Fair and Accurate Credit Transactions Act of 2003 at 5, December 2012., *available at* http://www.ftc.gov/sites/default/files/documents/reports/section-319-fair-and-accurate-credit-transactions-act-2003-fifth-interim-federal-trade-commission/130211factareport.pdf.

[18] The May 2011 study on credit reporting accuracy by the Policy and Economic Research Council (PERC) also found similar results with small differences. For example, one in five credit reports (19 percent) were alleged by consumers to have one or more potential inaccuracies on their records. In the PERC study, 1,970 potential inaccuracies (potentially material and not material) were identified in the 3,876 reports examined. See Michael Turner, Robin Varghese & Patrick D. Walker, PERC Results and Solutions, U.S. Consumer Credit Reports: Measuring Accuracy and Dispute Impacts (2011) *available at* http://www.perc.net/wp-content/uploads/2013/09/DQreport.pdf.

[19] The percentage of all credit report tradelines we estimated to represent accounts in collection in our 2012 white paper is larger than the 9.1 percent of tradelines we identify as collections tradelines in the Bureau's CCP. The 2012 figure represents the average of responses to a question submitted to all three NCRAs regarding the percentage of tradelines that represent accounts in collections; responses from the three NCRAs differed. In addition, our question did not narrowly define an account in collection as narrowly as we do here (where we define a collections tradeline as an account reported carrying a specific designation as defined in NCRA furnisher guidelines). The 2012 figure may include accounts that are severely delinquent and may have experienced a charge-off, but have not been furnished as collections tradelines.

[20] Consumer Financial Protection Bureau, Key Dimensions and Processes in the U.S. Credit Reporting System: A review of how the nation's largest credit bureaus manage consumer data at 29 (September 2012) *available at* http://files.consumerfinance.gov/f/201212_cfpb_credit-reporting-white-paper.pdf.

- The Federal Trade Commission's (FTC) December 2012 accuracy study found that collections tradelines accounted for 41 percent of the potential or alleged material errors identified by consumers on their credit reports and 40 percent of errors that were modified following disputes.[21] In addition, consumers who examined their credit reports in conjunction with the FTC's accuracy study had difficulty understanding how collections were reported; collection agencies did not generally identify the specific creditor or delinquent account that was involved.[22, 23] Again, the high error rate raises concern about the underlying accuracy of collections reporting.

- About 39 percent of consumer complaints received by the Bureau regarding collections practices are about inaccurate information or inaccurate claims pertaining to the account.[24] Of these, the most common complaint is that the consumer does not recognize the debt as his or hers (see Section 4, Table 4F). These complaints suggest that either the consumers are confused or mistaken about their accounts, or that the collectors are collecting on the wrong consumer or amount. To the extent the latter is true, such inaccuracies would presumably be incorporated into the information the collectors furnish to the NCRAs.

- Through its supervisory examinations of larger participants in the debt collections industry, the Bureau found that one or more large collectors systematically failed to investigate disputes from consumers received directly or through the NCRAs' e-OSCAR dispute handling system. In one example, the collector was simply removing the tradeline referenced in the dispute entirely from the files it sent to the NCRAs, causing the tradeline to be deleted from the consumers' credit reports rather than conducting an

---

[21] Federal Trade Commission, Report to Congress under Section 319 of the Fair and Accurate Credit Transactions Act of 2003, December 2012., *available at* http://www.ftc.gov/sites/default/files/documents/reports/section-319-fair-and-accurate-credit-transactions-act-2003-fifth-interim-federal-trade-commission/130211factareport.pdf.

[22] *Id.*

[23] To the extent that information about the identity of the creditor associated with collections tradelines on a credit report is unavailable, consumers will be more likely to dispute them as an error. See footnote 21.

[24] This percentage was calculated by summing all collection complaints with the following codes: "debt is not mine," "debt was paid," "attempted to collect wrong amount," or "debt was discharged in bankruptcy."

investigation.[25] In February 2014, the CFPB published Bulletin 2014-01, confirming furnishers' obligation under the FCRA to conduct investigations of disputes they receive from consumers.[26,27]

- In a public roundtable for industry and other stakeholders jointly hosted by the CFPB and the FTC in 2013, participants acknowledged the general lack of standard record-keeping practices used by debt collectors, debt buyers, and original creditors who assign or sell collections accounts to these entities. The lack of standards regarding what information is required to be present to substantiate a debt, and who is required to maintain it, could also introduce variability or inaccuracy to the credit reporting system when collectors or debt buyers furnish information about these accounts to the NCRAs.[28]

These concerns about the accuracy of information furnished by debt collectors and their treatment of disputes about the information carry particular weight given the negative impact such information can have on the credit standing and credit scores of consumers.

1.3   The special case of medical debt

Medical debts comprise roughly half (52 percent) of the collections tradelines that appear on consumer credit reports. Medical debts occur and are collected through unique circumstances and practices that amplify concerns raised about collections tradelines generally. In particular, the complexity of medical billing and the third-party reimbursement processes faced by most

---

[25] Consumer Financial Protection Bureau, Supervisory Highlights at 13 (Spring 2014) *available at* http://files.consumerfinance.gov/f/201405_cfpb_supervisory-highlights-spring-2014.pdf.

[26] Consumer Financial Protection Bureau, Bulletin 2014-01, (2014) *available at* http://files.consumerfinance.gov/f/201402_cfpb_bulletin_fair-credit-reporting-act.pdf.

[27] A collections tradeline that contains potentially inaccurate information and that is simply deleted without an investigation could result in same potential inaccuracy appearing in another tradeline on the consumer's credit report when the creditor reassigns the account to another debt collector. For further discussion about the impact of reassignment, see Section 3.

[28] Federal Trade Commission & Consumer Financial Protection Bureau, Roundtable on Data Integrity in Debt Collection: Life of a Debt (2013), *available at* http://www.ftc.gov/system/files/documents/public_events/71120/life-debt-roundtable-transcript.pdf.

patients and their families is a potential source of confusion or misunderstanding between patient, medical provider, and insurer. That complexity could lead some consumers to be unaware of when, to whom, or for what amount they owe a medical bill or even whether payment was the responsibility of the consumer rather than an insurance company.

While medical collections tradelines on credit reports appear as a result of circumstances that differ significantly from other types of collections tradelines, credit scoring models have until recently weighted such items identically to non-medical collections.[29] In a Data Point issued in May 2014, the CFPB examined how medical tradelines reflect the creditworthiness of consumers when compared to other types of collections tradelines. The report found that the presence of a medical collections tradeline on a credit report is less predictive of future defaults or serious delinquencies than the presence of a non-medical collections tradeline.[30]

1.4 Analysis of non-medical and medical collections tradelines on credit reports

This paper reflects findings from recent research by the CFPB to better quantify and understand how and when medical and non-medical collections tradelines appear on credit reports. Our research has involved analysis of data obtained from the CFPB's CCP, review of consumer complaints made to the CFPB pertaining to collections, interviews with collectors of medical and

---

[29] According to FICO, medical collections are scored by the FICO 8 model the same as any other type of collection on a consumer credit report. The company's latest model, FICO 9, weights medical and non-medical collections tradelines differently. Interview with FICO, in Washington, D.C. (Oct. 18, 2012).

[30] The authors found that consumers with more medical than non-medical collections tradelines had comparable delinquency rates to consumers whose scores were 8 to 10 points higher, but whose collections were mostly non-medical. They also demonstrated that consumers with paid medical debt experienced delinquency rates that were well below levels experienced by other consumers with the same scores whose medical collections were mostly unpaid. This pattern of over-performance was consistent over the entire score range. Consumers with paid medical debt were substantially over-penalized for their paid medical collections, with the median score differential ranging between 16 and 22 points. See Kenneth P. Brevoort & Michelle Kambara, Data Point: "Medical Debt and Credit Scores (May 2014), *available at* http://files.consumerfinance.gov/f/201405_cfpb_report_data-point_medical-debt-credit-scores.pdf.

non-medical debt and healthcare providers, and a review of literature on the medical billing and collections process.

We present analyses from the CCP in Section 2 to characterize the incidence and types of collections tradelines on credit reports. Section 3 discusses how collectors furnish the collections tradelines found on credit reports, the diversity of furnishing behavior, and how this can reflect the collectors' relationship with original creditors.

Section 4 focuses on medical collections tradelines on credit reports, and some ways in which consumers with medical collections exhibit different credit characteristics from consumers with non-medical collections. This section draws on interviews with collectors and healthcare providers to explore unique features of how medical debt arises and how it is collected and reported.

Section 5 summarizes the implications of our research findings concerning collections tradelines on credit reports and medical collections in particular. We discuss recent developments in credit scoring models that could result in more precise and nuanced judgments regarding consumers' creditworthiness based on the presence of collections tradelines, and ultimately benefit consumers.

2. The incidence and type of collections tradelines on credit reports

Approximately 220 million consumers' credit activity is reflected on credit files maintained by the three largest NCRAs.[31] In our sample of credit reports from one NCRA, collections tradelines appear on the credit reports of almost one third (31.6 percent) of consumers.

The incidence of different types of collections tradelines on consumers' credit reports in our sample is depicted in Table 1.[32] Nearly one in five consumers (19.5 percent) has a credit report containing one or more collections tradelines that originated with a medical provider.[33] Almost one out of every four consumers (24.5 percent) has one or more non-medical collections tradelines.

---

[31] See footnote 2.

[32] This study relies on guidance classifications provided to debt collection agencies and other furnishers by the CDIA under its "Metro®" guidelines for furnishers to the NCRAs. These guidelines classify debt collections tradelines into fifteen broad categories based on the original creditor's type of business. We report the largest of these business categories.

[33] This estimate of the percentage of consumers affected and our subsequent estimate of the share of collections tradelines on credit reports understate the impact of medical debt on consumers' credit reports. Our analysis does not account for or identify when a consumer has used a loan to pay medical bills. (For example, it is not uncommon for consumers to pay for their medical bills using their credit cards.)

TABLE 1: INCIDENCE OF COLLECTIONS TRADELINES

Collections tradeline type	Percentage of consumer credit reports containing one or more collections tradelines originating from...
Medical or health care	19.4%
Cable, cellular, wireless, other telecommunications	8.7%
Utilities or energy	7.6%
Retail collections	6.9%
Banking	2.7%
Financial	1.5%

The non-medical collections tradelines that originated from telecommunication companies (cable, landline, and wireless carriers) occur on 8.7 percent of credit reports; utilities (electric, water, and gas companies) occur on 7.6 percent; and retail stores occur on 6.9 percent of consumers' credit reports. Collections tradelines from finance companies represent debts owed primarily to non-auto and non-retail installment lenders; these were observed on 1.5 percent of our sample of credit reports. Collections accounts originating from banking creditors (primarily credit card accounts that are reported as collections tradelines) appeared on 2.7 percent of credit reports. [34] Education collections tradelines, predominately made up of student loans, appeared to affect less than 1 percent of consumers' credit reports. [35,36]

---

[34] The low share of consumers who have certain types of collections tradelines on their credit reports (and the low share of collections tradelines that are originated by certain types of creditors) may reflect differences in how some collection agencies and lenders report accounts that are severely delinquent. Some lenders do not report accounts that have been charged off and/or are in collections as collections tradelines to the NCRAs. For example, we observed a low incidence of credit card accounts being reported as in collections. Preliminary CFPB research has found that fewer than 17 percent of credit card accounts that have been charged off are reported as collections tradelines; of these, third-party collection agencies furnish 16 percent and credit card lenders 1 percent. This research indicates that most credit card accounts that have been charged off are reported by their original creditor as active tradelines that are either in extended delinquency or as having been charged off. These accounts are not counted among our estimate of total collections tradelines. Including seriously delinquent credit card accounts

Most consumers whose credit reports contain collections tradelines have multiple collections tradelines on their reports. The median consumer with collections tradelines has three such tradelines (with an average of 4.5 collections tradelines) on his or her report. Among the 19.5 percent of consumers who have medical collections tradelines, the median consumer has two such tradelines. Among the 24.5 percent of consumers who have non-medical collections tradelines on credit reports, the median consumer has two such tradelines (and an average of 2.8).

Looking across all collections tradelines, more than half (52.1 percent) are associated with medical providers. Figure 1 depicts the composition of all collections tradelines on credit reports by creditor type.

that have not yet been charged off, or seriously delinquent or charged off student loan debt, would further increase our estimate by an undetermined amount.

[35] For defaulted federal student loans, there are alternatives to sending a tradeline to a collection agency. These include withholding money from a consumer's tax refund or other federal payments, wage garnishment, or federal salary offset programs. Federal Student Aid Office, U.S. Department of Education *available at* https://studentaid.ed.gov/repay-loans/default/collections.

[36] Student loans that are severely delinquent appear to be similarly under-represented among collections tradelines. We have not estimated the portion of such loans that are reported as active tradelines by their original creditors or servicers.

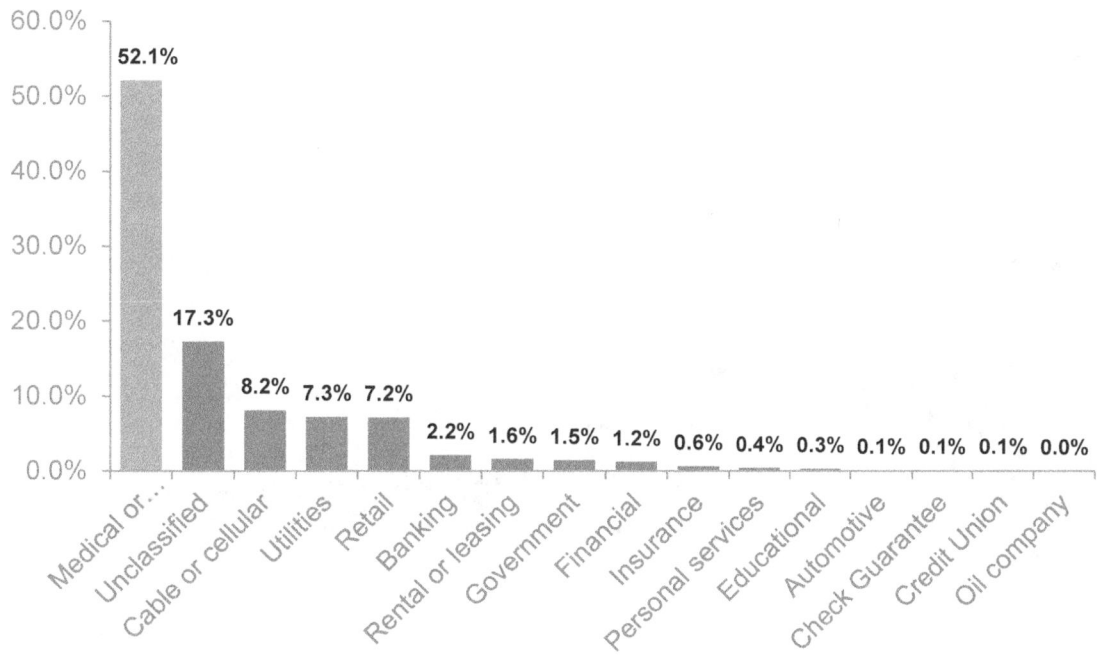

The collections tradelines observed in our sample are for small amounts, with a median amount owed of $270 and an average of $781. Eighty-five percent of collections tradelines are for amounts owed under $1,000. [37] A small number of very large unpaid collections tradelines account for the majority of total dollars reported in collections. The largest 10 percent of collections tradelines account for 61 percent of all dollars owed on collections tradelines, while the largest one percent of collections tradelines account for 25 percent of total collections amounts reported.

As Figure 2 indicates, the average and median amounts owed on collections; the amounts vary considerably by type of creditor.

---

[37] For some types of tradelines, the amount owed will reflect increases from the original balance of the debt owed, when interest and fees accrue on the original debt. Increasing balances occur most frequently among finance company accounts, where 48 percent these collections tradelines see regular increases in the monthly amount due.

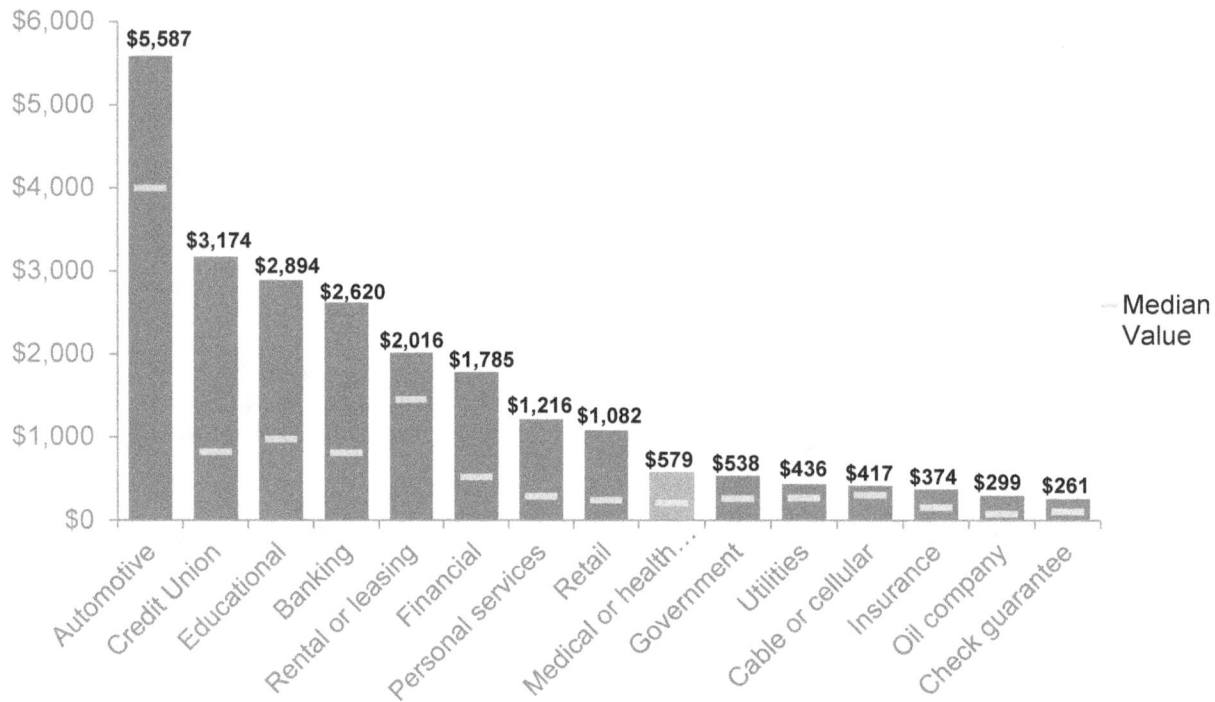

Although many consumers in the sample have medical collections tradelines on their credit reports, these debts often represent small amounts relative to the size of other types of debts. The average amount of a medical collections tradeline is $579 with a median of $207. About 75 percent of all medical collections are under $490. Utilities and telecommunications collections tradelines are similarly small.[38] In comparison, collections tradelines by finance companies average $1,785 with a median of $515. Automotive collections tradelines average $5,587 with a median of $3,995.[39] Overall, the average tradeline balance observed for all non-medical collections was $1,000 and the median was $366.

---

[38] These averages and medians are computed from all tradelines marked as collections tradelines. A few large tradelines can be considered outliers. For example, removing the top 1 percent of medical collections tradelines in our sample reduces the average amount of these collections tradelines to $315 from $579.

[39] Collection industry interviews suggest automotive collections tradeline amounts represent deficiencies remaining after vehicles have been repossessed by the creditor and the remaining debt has been assigned to a debt collector or sold to a debt buyer.

3. Furnishing behavior of debt collectors

The appearance of one or more collections tradelines above a minimum amount on a consumer's credit report has been viewed as a strong signal that the consumer may be experiencing difficulty in meeting his or her financial obligations, but this signal can be imprecise. As Section 2 suggests, collections tradelines can represent a diverse range of sizes and types of accounts that have become delinquent. This section further describes ways in which the appearance of collections tradelines can reflect diversity among debt collector furnishing practices and of creditor strategies to collect on a debt.

3.1 Diversity of collections furnishers

Collection agencies that furnish information about debts in collections to the NCRAs are numerous and diverse. In addition to variations in the size and in the types of accounts they handle, collections furnishers can be either contingency collection agencies or debt buyers.

- Contingency collection agencies are temporarily assigned responsibility for collecting by the owner of that debt, typically the original creditor. These companies generally receive a commission based on the number or amount of debts collected. Interviews with several collection agencies indicate commission amounts can range from 10 percent to 40 percent of the collectedamount, depending on the type and age of the debt.[40]

---

[40] Telephone interviews with collection agencies, in Washington, D.C., various dates (on file with CFPB).

- Debt buyers purchase collections accounts from original creditors or other buyers at a fraction of the face value of the total amount owed. Any amount collected above this purchase price is then realized as net revenue. Debt buyers can collect for themselves, rely on third-party collectors to pursue repayments, or enlist legal counsel to obtain judgments in court.

Compared to furnishing by the financial firms that account for the majority of active tradelines in credit reports, the furnishing of collections tradelines by debt collectors (both contingency firms and debt buyers) is fragmented. The Bureau's 2012 whitepaper on credit reporting found that the 10 largest furnishers by tradeline count contributed more than half of all active tradelines reported to the NCRAs.[41] In contrast, the largest furnisher of collections tradelines in our national sample of credit reports is responsible for reporting only 4.7 percent of such tradelines, and the top 10 furnishers for 22.1 percent. We can identify approximately 1,400 different entities that furnish collections account information.[42]

The degree of fragmentation varies significantly by the type of debt in collections. Table 2 depicts the share of tradelines in our sample reported by the largest three furnishers and top 10 furnishers for major categories of debt. Medical debt reporting is highly fragmented, with the top 10 furnishers accounting for only 18 percent of medical collections tradelines. In contrast, the top 10 furnishers in the utilities, telecommunications, finance company, banking, and retail industries account for between 59 percent and 83 percent of collections tradelines in those industries.

---

[41] Consumer Financial Protection Bureau, Key Dimensions and Processes in the U.S. Credit Reporting System: A review of how the nation's largest credit bureaus manage consumer data (September 2012) *available at* http://files.consumerfinance.gov/f/201212_cfpb_credit-reporting-white-paper.pdf.

[42] The Bureau estimates there are 4,500 debt collection agencies in the U.S.; however, we are unable to determine from our sample of credit reports the percentage of these agencies that furnish to the NCRAs. See Defining Larger Participants in Certain Consumer Financial Product and Service Markets, 77 Fed. Reg. 9592 (Feb. 17, 2012), *available at* https://www.federalregister.gov/articles/2012/02/17/2012-3775/defining-larger-participants-in-certain-consumer-financial-product-and-service-markets#p-100.

TABLE 2: PERCENTAGE OF COLLECTIONS TRADELINES ATTRIBUTED TO TOP FURNISHERS BY TYPE

Collections tradeline type	Top furnisher tradeline share	Second largest furnisher tradeline share	Third largest furnisher tradeline share	Top 10 furnishers' tradeline share
Medical/ Health Care Collections	3.1%	2.5%	2.3%	18.3%
Cable, Cellular and Wireless Collections	36.9%	13.1%	12.3%	83.2%
Utilities and Energy Collections	32.4%	15.6%	3.5%	66.1%
Financial Collections	36.2%	15.8%	4.6%	74.3%
Banking Collections	29.7%	23.1%	22.3%	87.1%
Retail Collections	20.7%	9.8%	7.0%	58.9%

3.2 Variations in the timing of collections tradeline reporting

The first appearance of most collections tradelines on credit reports begins with the decision by a creditor either to assign the debt to a third-party collector (and accord the collector responsibility for furnishing to the NCRAs) or to sell the account to a debt buyer, which begins furnishing information about the account. This decision can occur at a variety of different points in the life of the account and stages of delinquency.

The creditor can choose to assign or sell the accounts at any stage of delinquency. In some cases, the assignment can occur prior to charge-off. In some industries such as utilities or healthcare, the timing of when a creditor can assign accounts to a third-party collector can be governed by state laws or regulations.[43] Industry interviews suggest that in the highly fragmented market for medical collections where collections practices vary widely, assignment of unpaid medical bills to third-party debt collectors can even occur when the bills are only 60 or even just 30 days past due. Generally, when collectors furnish information to the NCRAs about these accounts, the collections tradelines that result can represent delinquencies at a variety of stages.

There is similar variation in timing as to when a creditor chooses to sell an account to a debt buyer. Industry interviews suggest that most sales to debt buyers only occur after an account has been charged off by the original creditor. But sale - and subsequent furnishing of an account as a collections tradeline by the buyer - can occur immediately after charge-off, or months or years later.

Because of these variations, there is only a limited relationship between the severity or "recency" of the delinquency and the timing a collections tradeline first appears on a consumer's credit report. NCRA guidelines instruct furnishers to include the date of first delinquency when furnishing information about collections tradelines. This date should enable a user of a credit report to determine the severity of delinquency of a collections tradeline when it first appears. However, the date of first delinquency is not always available to the archived credit report information that score developers use to develop and test their models. Some models therefore can not take the date of first delinquency into account when determining the weight accorded a collections tradeline in a consumer's credit score.[44]

---

[43] One survey of a small sample of utility companies about their collections and credit reporting practices has found that utilities vary considerably as to the stage of delinquency at which they transfer accounts to third-party collection agencies and when those agencies pass on these delinquencies and defaults to the NCRAs. PERC: "Credit Reporting Customer Payment Data: Impact on Customer Payment Behavior and Furnisher Costs and Benefits;" 2009 at 17-19 *available at* http://www.perc.net/wp-content/uploads/2013/09/bizcase_0.pdf.

[44] Not all NCRAs can provide the date of first delinquency in the archived data. It is the archived data that model developers use to create credit scores.

3.3 Variations in tradeline persistence and fall-off

The variety of strategies creditors use when engaging collection agencies to recover or liquidate defaulted debt is also reflected in variations in the duration of collections tradelines on credit reports. Figure 3 illustrates the persistence of a single "vintage" of collections tradelines on credit reports over an 18-month period. [45] The persistence of each tradeline varies by type of account. For some types of accounts, most tradelines that first appeared at the beginning of the observation period were no longer reported by the furnisher at the end of the period. The observed fall-off was greatest among telecommunications, utilities, and retail tradelines.[46]

FIGURE 3:   PERSISTANCE OF FRESH COLLECTIONS TRADELINES BY TYPE

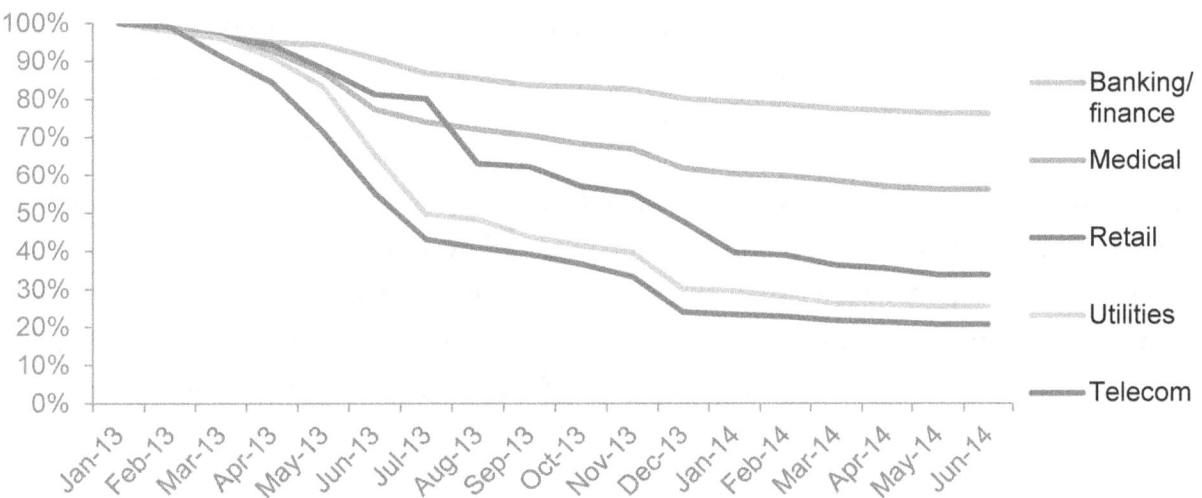

---

[45] A "vintage" of credit accounts generally refers to accounts or loans that were originated at the same point in time. Here we use the term "vintage" to refer to collections tradelines that first appeared on consumers' credit reports at the same point in time from a particular furnisher. Collections tradelines of the same vintage herein may represent credit accounts that were originated at different points of time or became delinquent on different dates. The particular vintage of accounts referred to in the analysis we describe first appeared as fresh collections tradelines in January 2013 and were tracked through June 2014.

[46] For the purposes of this study, we designate the term "fall-off" to mean that the tradeline disappeared from the record during the 18-month period observed and was not aged off the record as per the maximum reporting time allowed under the FCRA.

We believe that re-assignment of accounts by creditors among multiple contingency collection agencies explains most of the tradeline "fall-off" from the consumer's record. Interviews with collection agencies and other industry observers indicate that to maximize recoveries, many creditors assign their delinquent accounts to a collection agency for a limited period of time and then re-assign accounts from which the first agency has been unable to collect to a second collection agency. As a result, the collectors first report information about these accounts to the NCRAs at or after the beginning of the contract period during which their client creditors assign them to collect on these accounts. Following the end of this assignment period, guidelines published by the NCRAs require the collector to cease reporting and remove information on these accounts from the NCRAs' files. After the accounts have been re-assigned, the new collection agency may begin reporting information about the accounts to the NCRAs, resulting in a new collections tradeline appearing in the consumers' credit report.[47]

Some large creditors can have tiers of collectors: a primary tier to which it initially assigns a portfolio of debts, a secondary tier of collectors to which it assigns debts after they have been unsuccessfully "worked" for a period of time, and even a tertiary tier to which older debts are assigned (if they are not eventually sold to a debt buyer).

We hypothesize that fall-off is relatively limited in the banking and finance industries because many collections tradelines in these industries are reported by debt buyers. Historically, credit card debts have accounted for the largest share of debt buyer purchases; these accounts are then categorized as "banking" collections tradelines on credit reports.[48] These tradelines exhibited the lowest occurrence of fall-off. This could reflect the tendency of these debt buyers to hold purchased debts for long periods.

Fall-off of medical collections is relatively low when compared with other types of collections tradelines. This can be explained by relatively low rates of debt reassignment by medical providers. Interviews suggest that many medical providers choose not to manage multiple

---

[47] The data contained in our sample of credit reports does not make it feasible to easily track tradelines that drop off at the end of collections assignment periods and then re-appear when reported by a new collector. We have not estimated what percentage of such tradelines reappear or what period of time typically transpires before they do.

[48] Federal Trade Commission, The Structure and Practices of the Debt Buying Industry (2013), *available at* http://www.ftc.gov/sites/default/files/documents/reports/structure-and-practices-debt-buying-industry/debtbuyingreport.pdf.

collector relationships. They tend to contract with a small number of contingency collectors from which they do not subsequently re-assign their accounts.

The impact of re-assignment is more evident when observing vintages of accounts from individual furnishers. Figures 4-9 illustrates the January 2013 vintage of accounts reported by the largest individual furnishers in the medical, telecommunications, banking, retail, utility, and finance industries. Account fall-off within each of these industries is quite varied. In addition, many of these accounts fall-off in steep "cliffs" that occur 3, 4, 6, or 12 months from the time they first appear on the consumer's record. These "cliffs" likely represent the end of assignment periods.[49]

Gradual slopes between cliffs, or in the absence of cliffs, can represent deletion of accounts over time. We hypothesize that this gradual fall-off can result from a combination of disputes from consumers, aging off of debts that have exceeded the seven year obsolescence period and deletion of some accounts after they have been repaid.

FIGURE 4: COLLECTIONS TRADELINE PERSISTANCE OF LARGEST FURNISHERS FOR MEDICAL

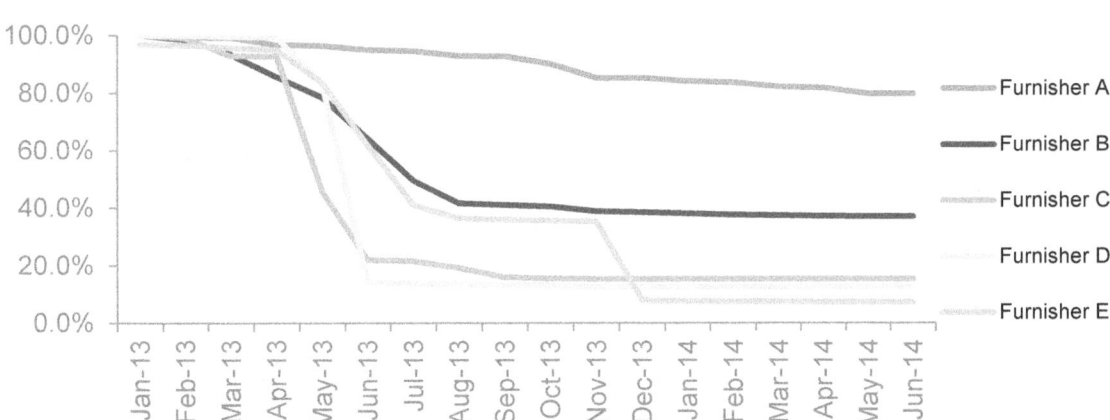

---

[49] We also hypothesize that the large furnishers with gradual fall-off slopes and no cliffs may represent debt buyers who collect on debts that they have purchased and who are not subject to assignment periods from creditors.

FIGURE 5: COLLECTIONS TRADELINE PERSISTANCE OF LARGEST FURNISHERS FOR TELECOM

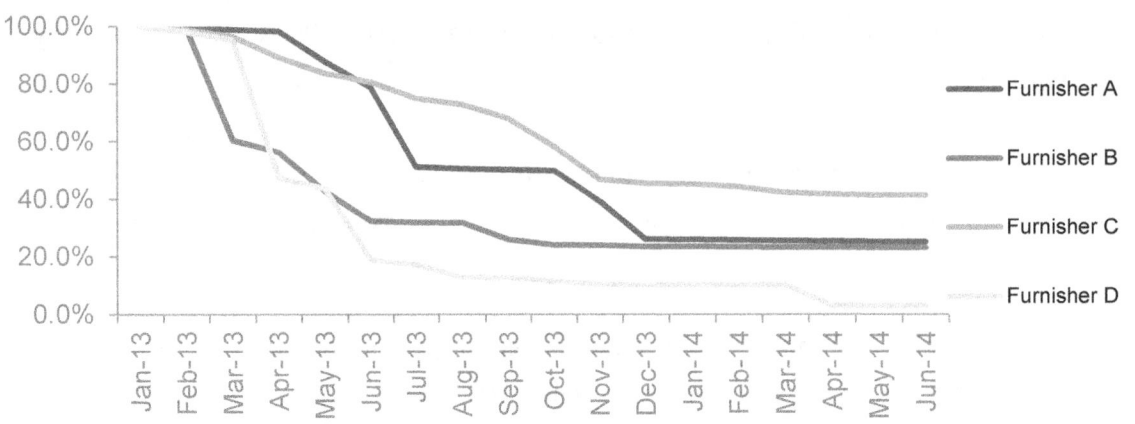

FIGURE 6: COLLECTIONS TRADELINE PERSISTANCE OF LARGEST FURNISHERS FOR FINANCE

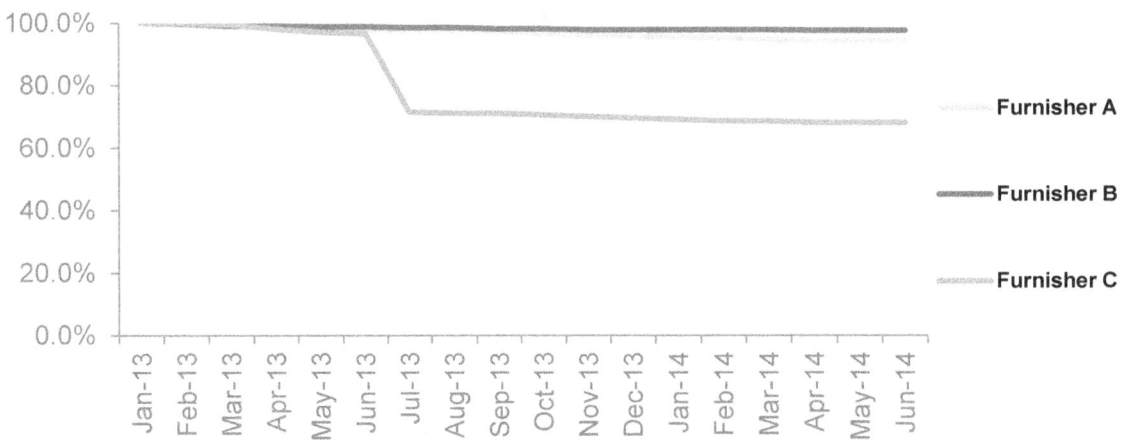

FIGURE 7: COLLECTIONS TRADELINE PERSISTANCE OF LARGEST FURNISHERS FOR RETAIL

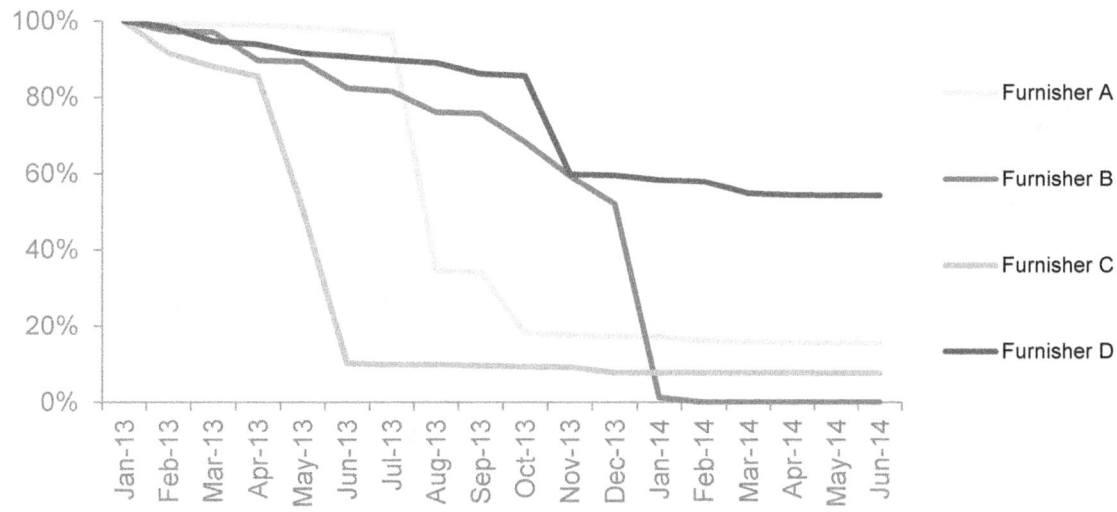

FIGURE 8: COLLECTIONS TRADELINE PERSISTANCE OF LARGEST FURNISHERS BY BANKING
FURNISHERS

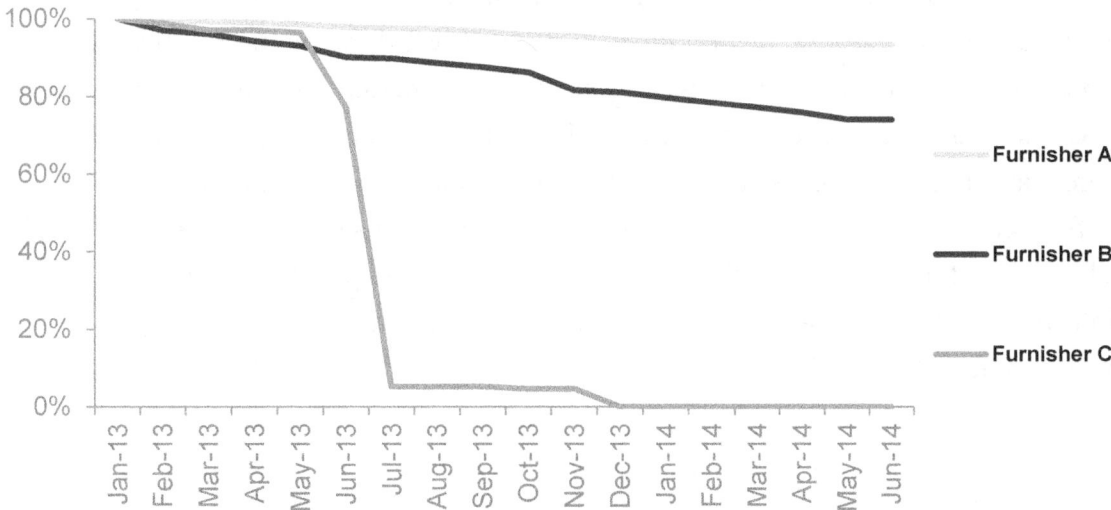

FIGURE 9: COLLECTIONS TRADELINE PERSISTANCE OF LARGEST FURNISHERS BY UTILITY FURNISHERS

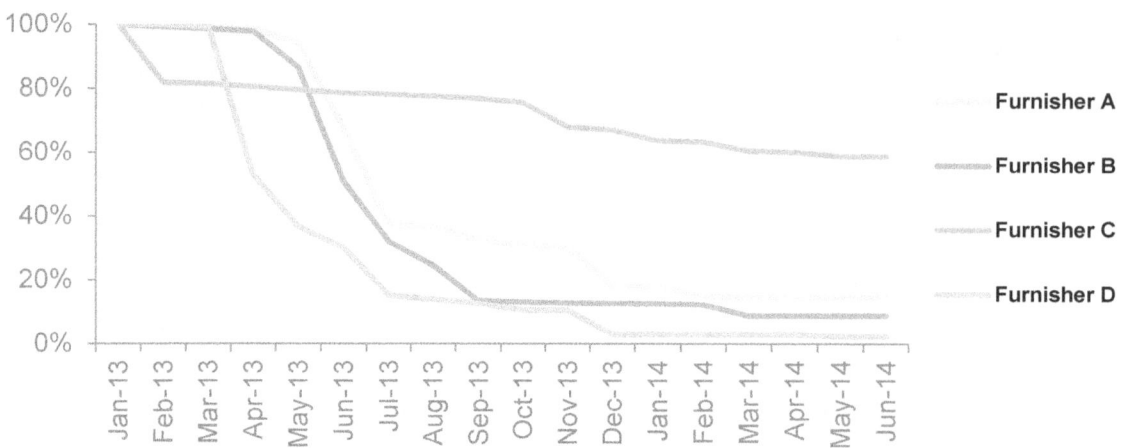

In recent interviews conducted during research on this paper, contingency collection agencies stated that when they receive a request for validation from consumers under section 809 of the Fair Debt Collection Practices Act or a dispute from consumers regarding the accuracy of tradeline information under section 623 of the FCRA, they forward the request or dispute to the original creditor.[50],[51] During the dispute process, furnishers state that they remove the tradeline from the consumer's credit report until they can verify that the account is valid or that the furnished information is accurate. We are not able to determine from our sample data whether the firms or their client creditors conduct the required investigations under these statutes or, if investigated and found to be correct, if the collector-furnishers re-report the validated or corrected information. Nor can we determine or quantify the extent to which fall-off is attributable to disputes or other causes.

---

[50] 15 U.S.C. § 1692g (2012).

[51] 15 U.S.C. § 1681s-2 (2012).

3.4 Changes in status or balance of collections

Consumer reporting industry guidelines instruct furnishers to report when a tradeline has been paid in full or settled for less than the full balance by noting "paid" and indicating that the balance owed is $0.[52] Our sample of collections tradelines that first appeared in January of 2013 indicates that the rates at which accounts are converted to "paid" varies considerably by account type, as seen in Figure 10. While an average of 6.7 percent of collections tradelines are converted to paid, this conversion rate can vary from 4.1 percent in the telecom industry to 11.8 percent in the banking industry.

---

[52] A "paid" status refers to collections tradelines that have been marked as "paid in full" or "settled for less than full balance."

FIGURE 10: PAID OR SETTLED IN FULL RATES BY TYPE OF COLLECTIONS TRADELINE

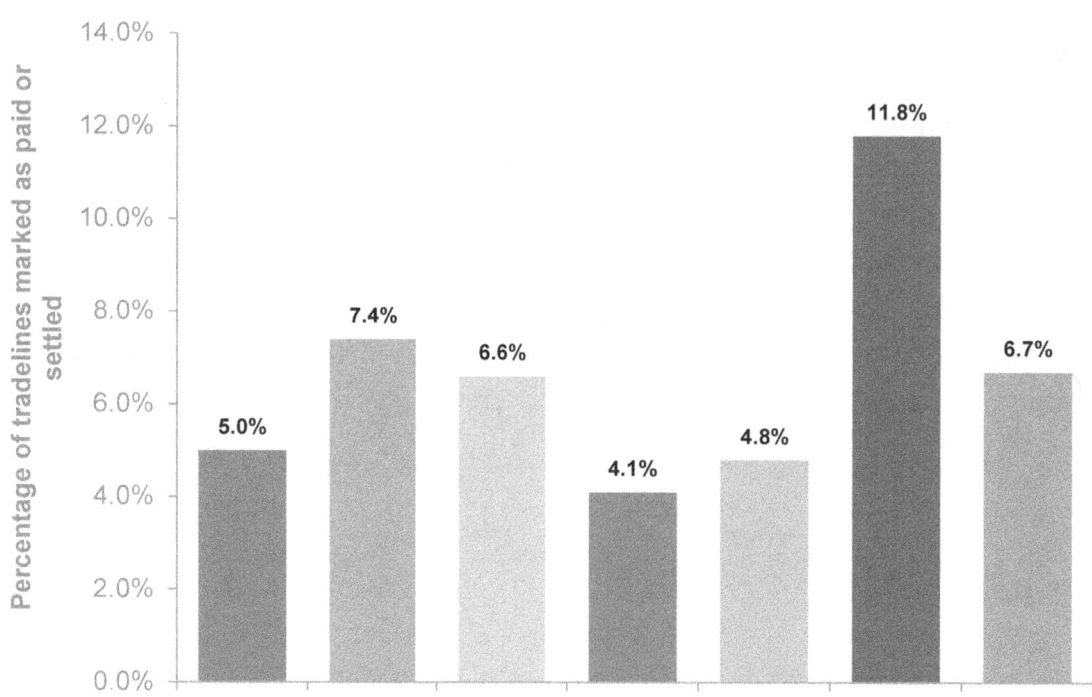

The variations between account types in the rate of settlement partly reflects differences in the effectiveness of collections efforts, which can in turn reflect differences in the nature of the debts (for example, difference in the ages at which debts are sent to collectors between industries), or differences across the consumers who owe these debts. The variation in settlement rates can also reflect differences in furnishing practices across industries. NCRA reporting guidelines instruct furnishers to continue to report collections accounts that have been closed and settled until the FCRA obsolescence date has been reached.[53] [54] However, our data do not allow us to assess how consistently this requirement is being met by collections tradeline furnishers.

---

[53] See footnote 13.

[54] As per the Fair Credit Reporting Act, information excluded from consumer reports include accounts placed for collection or charged to profit and loss which antedate the report by more than seven years. The seven year period "[...] shall begin, with respect to any delinquent account that is placed for collection (internally or by referral to a

3.5 Account updating

Industry guidelines for reporting to the NCRAs instruct furnishers to update information on all accounts every month.[55] We observed that while most lenders furnishing data on active tradelines observe this reporting standard, most collectors furnishing collections tradelines do not.

During a six month period from December 2013 to June 2014, only a small fraction of medical, utilities, and telecom collections tradelines were updated on a regular monthly basis. The majority were never updated during this time period. In comparison, the large majority of active (i.e. non-collections) tradelines are updated on a regular basis.

Furnishers of financial and banking collections accounts updated information of their tradelines regularly. This updating behavior can relate to the fact that banking and finance items are largely revolving or installment credit accounts that can be subject to ongoing interest and other fees that collectors are permitted to accrue under state law and/or under the terms of the original credit contract; furnishers of these items can be motivated to update on a regular basis in order to maintain accurate information about the changing balances owned in the consumers' files. It is unclear why medical, utilities, and telecom collections tradelines are not updated on a monthly basis.

3.6 Furnishing as collections strategy

Furnishing information to the NCRAs can provide an incentive for borrowers or debtors to meet their repayment obligations. Reporting derogatory information such as a collections tradeline may motivate the consumer to contact the collection agency to resolve the debt, but could also harm the consumer if the tradeline is reported without his/her knowledge, and/or if the

---

third party, whichever is earlier), charged to profit and loss, or subjected to any similar action, upon the expiration of the 180-day period beginning on the date of the commencement of the delinquency which immediately preceded the collection activity, charge to profit and loss, or similar action" 15 U.S.C. §1681c.

[55] As per CDIA Metro 2® guidelines, third party collection agencies and debt buyers should update accounts as "in collections" each month until the tradeline is paid. After payment, collections tradelines should be reported as "account pain in full, was a collection account".

consumer did not have prior knowledge of the debt. Lack of prior knowledge can be more prevalent in the case of medical debt due to the confusion caused by the medical billing process.

A collector may be most likely to resort to this tactic when the amount owed on a collections account is small. Small dollar accounts are most often observed for telecommunications, utility, and medical accounts. Attempts to make direct contact with the consumer via mail or telephone to collect may not be cost efficient based on the odds of recovery and the amounts recovered. Industry interviews have suggested that some collectors employ a strategy of "passive collections" that involves reporting a debt in collections to the NCRAs and simply waiting for the consumer to discover the tradeline (rather than actively seeking to collect from the consumer).[56] We cannot assess how often passive collections is used by collectors because we cannot determine from our research whether the consumer was informed of the debt before the collections tradeline was reported.

Whether or not a third-party collection agency reports to the NCRAs is generally a decision made by the creditor that assigns accounts for collection. Some creditors instruct their collectors to furnish. Others choose not to use furnishing as a collections strategy. Collectors told us in interviews that not all of their clients permit them to furnish account information. And some collectors whose clients have given them the option to furnish choose not to exercise that option.

The Healthcare Financial Management Association (HFMA) has stated that furnishing to a consumer reporting agency is a common practice in the hospital industry.[57] However, we interviewed several non-profit hospitals that do not allow their debt collectors to report to the NCRAs because they believe this behavior can damage their reputations within the communities they serve.

---

[56] Telephone interviews with collection agencies, in Washington, D.C., various dates (on file with CFPB).

[57] A 2005 HFMA survey shows that 83 percent of respondents (medical providers) report unpaid accounts to a consumer reporting agency. Sixty-seven percent responded that they report unpaid accounts of any amount, 16 percent report unpaid accounts over a certain amount, 13 percent do not report unpaid accounts, and 4 percent were unsure. Bureau interviews indicate that nearly all healthcare providers that permit reporting prefer to allow their contracted collection agencies to report the unpaid accounts to credit reporting agencies as opposed to reporting the unpaid accounts themselves. *See* Letter from Joseph Fifer, President and CEO Healthcare Financial Management Association, to Internal Revenue Service (September 24, 2012) *available at* www.hfma.org/WorkArea/linkit.aspx?LinkIdentifier=id&ItemID=5302.

Whether or not certain creditors permit their debt collectors to furnish collections account information to consumer reporting agencies may also be governed under state laws or regulations that pertain to utilities or healthcare providers. Regardless of the reasons, the fact that some collectors report while others do not introduces further variability into the marketplace as to when collections tradelines appear or do not appear on consumers' credit reports.

In general, whether or not a collections tradeline appears on a consumer's credit report, when it appears or disappears, and whether it is labeled as paid or deleted when the account is settled, all reflect furnishing policies and strategies of creditors and of the debt collection agencies and debt buyers with which they do business. These practices can vary considerably and introduce a range of variability that is not present in the reporting of active tradelines, for which payment status (*i.e.*, whether a payment is current, 30 days late, 60 days late, etc.) is the primary indicator of delinquency. This variability by industry, creditor, and furnisher makes the appearance of any given collections tradeline an imprecise indicator of a consumer's financial condition or willingness to repay and can reflect a variety of facts and circumstances. This imprecision is offset by the fact that most consumers who have a collections tradeline on their credit report have more than one (as outlined in Section 2) and often have other delinquent accounts (as discussed in Section 4). The more collections tradelines that appear, the more confidently a user can interpret their presence as indicators of financial distress, though this generalization holds less true for consumers who have multiple medical collections tradelines, as the next section will suggest.

4. Medical collections tradelines

The process of incurring medical expenses and the process by which such expenses are turned into medical bills differs from recurring bills from installment lenders, credit card companies, utilities, or telecommunications companies. Lack of price transparency and the complex system of insurance coverage and cost sharing means many consumers, including those who have health coverage, receive medical bills that are a source of confusion. As a result, they can incur medical debts in collections without certainty about what they owe, to whom, when, or for what. This uncertainty could affect any consumer, regardless of their financial condition. Our research on medical collections tradelines demonstrates that a large portion of consumers with medical debts in collections show no other evidence of financial distress and are consumers who ordinarily pay their other financial obligations on time.

4.1 US Consumers' medical payment obligations

The majority of U.S. consumers under age 65 and their children are covered under health insurance plans that they receive through employers.[58] Some consumers purchase health insurance policies directly from insurers for themselves and their families. Older Americans can receive coverage through the federal government's Medicare program. Many low-income Americans and their children are covered through state-administered Medicaid programs: both the consumer eligibility and treatment coverage vary by state. In 2013, a remaining 42 million

---

[58]The Bureau of Labor Statistics, Trends in employment-based health insurance coverage: evidence from the National Compensation Survey, Oct. 14, 2014, *available at* http://www.bls.gov/opub/mlr/2014/article/trends-in-employment-based-health-insurance-coverage.htm.

consumers had no health insurance and were responsible for paying providers for the full cost of healthcare they received.[59]

For consumers with some form of medical insurance, the billing process begins when the provider bills the consumer directly and the consumer seeks reimbursement from the insurer, or (more commonly) when the provider files claims with the consumer's insurer for the cost of the treatment. In the latter cases, once the insurer determines the amount of reimbursement, the provider then bills the consumer for the unreimbursed balance subject to any limitations that may have been agreed upon between the provider and the insurer. Most consumers with medical coverage are responsible for some portion of the billed cost of many types of care before or after obtaining medical treatment, until an annual out-of-pocket maximum on consumer payments is reached. Consumer obligations can take the form of co-payments for doctors' visits, the cost of drug prescriptions, or annual per-person and/or per-household deductible amounts the consumer must pay before insurance will begin coverage. These factors can determine a consumer's share of out-of-pocket expenses for a particular treatment.

4.1.1 Complexity and lack of transparency up front

Unlike credit cards, installment loans, utilities, or wireless or cable service that have contractual account disclosures describing terms and conditions of use,[60] most often consumers are not told the costs of medical services in advance. Consumers needing urgent or emergency care rarely know or are provided with the cost of a treatment or procedures beforehand.[61] Even in non-emergency situations, the specific treatments, tests, or procedures needed are regularly

---

[59] The percentage of people without health insurance for the entire year of 2013 was 13.4 percent (est. 42 million). (Jessica Smith & Carla Medalia, *Health Insurance Coverage in the United States: 2012, Current Population Reports,* Sept. 2014, *available at* http://www.census.gov/content/dam/Census/library/publications/2014/demo/p60-250.pdf).

[60] Some of these disclosures are required under federal or state laws or regulations. For example, requirements that consumers receive certain disclosure of credit terms are spelled out in the Truth in Lending Act, and its implementing Regulation Z (see http://files.consumerfinance.gov/f/201409_cfpb_tila-respa-integrated-disclosure-rule_compliance-guide.pdf). Some State laws or regulations require similar disclosures for utility or telecommunications service agreements.

[61] Tara Siegel Bernard, Getting Lost in the Labyrinth of Medical Bills, The New York Times, June 22, 2012, available at http://www.nytimes.com/2012/06/23/your-money/health-insurance/navigating-the-labyrinth-of-medical-costs-your-money.html?_r=0.

determined through diagnoses that occur at the time of treatment. When a consumer is hospitalized, physicians and hospitals often determine what sort of treatments a consumer needs, and administer them during a hospital stay.

Even if the treatment is known in advance, the provider's price and billed amount for that procedure might depend on which insurer covers that particular patient and the specific insurer's pre-negotiated pricing for that treatment.[62]

For many insurance plans, the share of the cost that the consumer must pay can vary depending on the type of treatment and whether the provider is within or outside of a network of preferred providers under the insurance plan. Consumers may have difficulty determining whether a provider is "in-network" or "out-of-network" in certain situations. This particularly occurs with emergency care when both in-network and out-of-network providers may serve patients. The consumer's obligation also can vary based upon whether the consumer has reached an annual cap on the amount the consumer can be required to pay out-of-pocket or whether the consumer's family has reached an annual family cap. This, too, can be difficult for a consumer to determine.

4.1.2   Complexity and lack of transparency post-treatment

For consumers who are insured and providers who accept the consumer's insurance, after treatment, the medical provider's billing department sends codes in the form of a claim to the insurer. A period of adjudication follows in which the insurer reviews the claim and determines whether the provider is eligible for payment; whether the specific claimed treatment is warranted under the diagnosis and fundable under the policy; whether the costs claimed match the provider's pre-negotiated rates with the insurer; and whether there is an applicable co-payment or deductible for which the consumer is responsible.

The consumer generally will receive an Explanation of Benefits (EOB) from the insurer noting what treatments have been claimed, the cost, the portion covered by the insurer, whether any treatments were received from out of network providers, and the amount of the unreimbursed balance remaining that will be the responsibility of the patient or his or her family to pay. Unless

---

[62] *Id.*

the claim is fully covered by the insurer or the provider has agreed to accept the insurance reimbursement as full payment, the established deductible and/or coinsurance amount will then be billed to the consumer by the provider. For treatments or procedures not covered by the insurer from out-of-network providers, the consumer is likely to receive a bill from the provider for the full amount of the treatment or the amount not covered by the claim (balance billing).[63]

The complexity of these processes and the resulting bills is exacerbated whenever multiple procedures and multiple providers are involved. For some procedures (for example, a surgery) it is common for consumers to receive bills from multiple providers (for example, the surgeon, the anesthesiologist, and the surgery facility).[64] A consumer may also receive multiple bills from the same provider when the provider bills the consumer before the insurer has completed its review and adjudication of the provider's claim. When treatments involve multiple visits, each can result in a separate bill or series of bills.

A consumer who lacks insurance coverage faces a billing process that is less complex, but the amounts owed are not likely to be subject to greater up-front price transparency. The uninsured consumer can be billed immediately after treatment and will likely receive a bill that is for the full cost of the treatment.[65] The uninsured consumer can experience significant variation in price from provider to provider and market to market, and often may not receive the same prices from providers that insurers are able to negotiate.

In summary, for the consumer presented with bills and/or an EOB, there is potential for confusion around the procedure, the provider, the amount billed, and how much was covered by the insurer. The consumer can receive EOBs and bills months after the time of treatment and may be uncertain about what financial obligation he or she actually has. These sources of potential confusion increase the likelihood the consumer will hesitate or delay paying a medical provider's bill because the consumer does not recognize or understand the information contained on the bill. Considerations and questions might include whether the amount was

---

[63] Elisabeth Rosenthal, *After Surgery, Surprise $117,000 Medical Bill From Doctor He Didn't Know*, The New York Times, Sept. 20, 2014, *available at* http://www.nytimes.com/2014/09/21/us/drive-by-doctoring-surprise-medical-bills.html.

[64] Industry interview Children's National Medical Center, in Washington, D.C., Nov. 6, 2012.

[65] See footnote 64.

already paid by his or her insurance, whether the correct amount was billed, or whether the consumer actually received the billed treatment. With the combination of lack of price transparency and the third-party insurer's relationship with the different providers, the consumer is left with having to review each medical bill carefully and seek verification from providers or insurers when questions arise. [66]

4.2 Consumer complaints to the CFPB about medical collections

Consumer complaints to the CFPB regarding debt collections accounts provide some evidence of the confusion or uncertainty that can result from the medical billing process. Complaints from consumers who are subject to medical collections are more likely to be about amounts owed or whether or not the bill was paid as compared to complaints about other types of collections accounts.

The CFPB receives complaints directly from consumers through the CFPB website and other channels. Consumers categorize their complaints first by product or service provider type, and then by the nature of the complaint. A two-month sample period from May and June 2014 containing about 15,000 de-identified consumer complaints regarding debt collections was used to understand common concerns and review firsthand the consumers' issues relating to collections debt. From the collections complaints received in this period, we were able to identify a portion of complaints that were directly related to attempts to collect on medical accounts.[67]

---

[66] The Healthcare Financial Management Association (HFMA) notes "There is confusion among healthcare consumers about how to obtain clear, understandable pricing information. The differences among healthcare charges and prices and the widespread variations in service, quality, and outcomes all are shrouded in an air of uncertainty and complexity. The all-too-common result is misunderstanding."

Brian Workinger, Front-Line Perspectives on price Transparency and Estimation, HFM Magazine, Sept. 2014

[67] We identified collections complaints that were related to medical accounts by conducting a word search of consumers' narrative descriptions of their complaints. There are likely to be additional complaints that were about collections that pertained to medical accounts among the entire sample of collections complaints that we were

Consumers identifying as having medical debt were more than twice as likely to claim the "debt was paid" (20.1 percent for medical collections complaints compared to 8.4 percent for non-medical). These consumers were more likely to claim that they were "not given enough information to verify [the] debt" (14.5 percent of medical collections complaints compared to 9.0 percent of non-medical) or that the collector was "attempting to collect the wrong amount" (7.6 percent of medical compared to 4.7 percent of non-medical collections complaints). Complaints from consumers about medical collections were less likely to be about hostile or abusive communications from collectors (*i.e.*, frequent or repeated phone calls or threats of legal action) than were those from consumers with non-medical collections complaints.

4.3 The profile of consumers with medical debt collections

As previously noted, research performed by the CFPB demonstrated that credit scoring models that treat medical collections in the same way as other collections tradelines penalize consumers with medical debt collections by underestimating their creditworthiness with lower scores.[68] The study found that consumers with medical debt were more likely to pay their future loan obligations on par with consumers scoring at least ten points higher. In cases where the consumer's medical debt was paid off, the scores underestimated the consumer's creditworthiness by an average of 22 points.

As discussed above, the medical pricing, billing, and reimbursement process often lacks transparency and may engender consumer confusion or uncertainty. This in turn can cause some consumers who ordinarily pay their bills on time to delay or withhold payments on medical debts. This could explain why the presence of medical collections tradelines on a consumer's credit report can be a less reliable predictor of future delinquency than other types of collections accounts.

---

unable to differentiate because the narratives did not contain the search terms. Further, a significant proportion of collections-related complaints are about the practices of first party creditors, who also do not report the accounts they collect on directly as collections tradelines.

[68] Kenneth P. Brevoort & Michelle Kambara, Data Point: "Medical Debt and Credit Scores (May 2014), *available at* http://files.consumerfinance.gov/f/201405_cfpb_report_data-point_medical-debt-credit-scores.pdf.

To assess the extent to which consumers who incur medical collections tradelines differ from consumers who are subject to other types of collection activity, we analyzed the differences between the credit histories of consumers in three different groups: consumers who had only medical collections tradelines, those who only had non-medical collections tradelines, and those who had both types of debt on their credit reports. As Figure 11 indicates, roughly 7 percent of consumers have one or more medical collections tradelines on their credit reports with no other types of collections, 12.1 percent of consumers have only non-medical tradelines, and 12.3 percent have both.

FIGURE 11:   CONSUMER RECORDS WITH COLLECTIONS TRADELINES BY TYPE

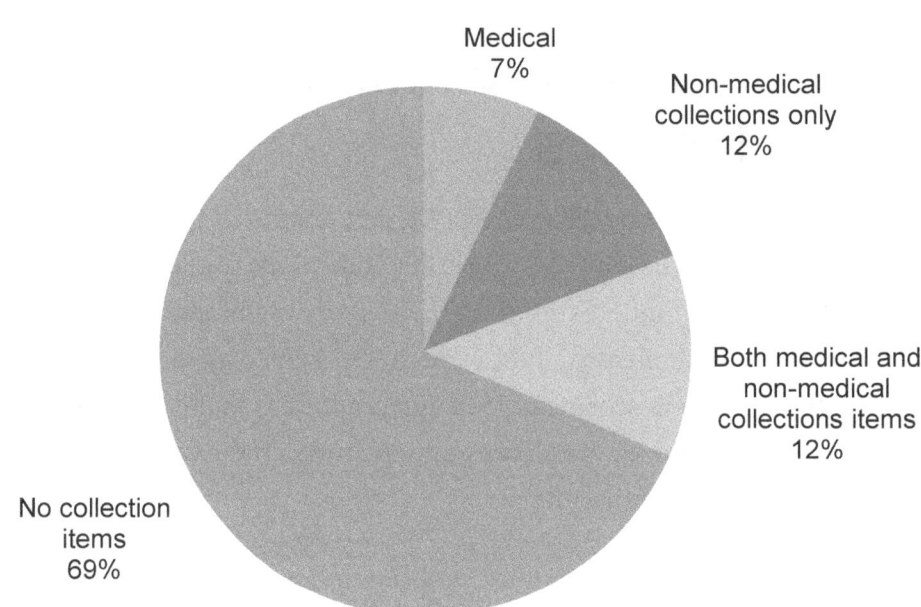

We observed that all three groups of consumers were more likely to have had a serious delinquency (defined as 60 or more days past due) among their active (*i.e.*, non-collections) tradelines than consumers with no collections debt reported. [69] We compared the worst non-

---

[69] Among consumers without any collections tradelines, 70 percent had no late payments at all on their records, and 12 percent had some occurrence of occasional 30-day delinquencies or one billing cycle late. By this definition we consider 82 percent of the non-collections control group to have "clean" records in their payment behavior. In comparison to this baseline, the proportion of non-medical collections consumers with "clean" records was only 37

collections delinquency among each consumer's active tradelines in all three groups. We broke out consumers in each group by the number of collections tradelines contained on their reports. We found that the proportion of each group we describe as "clean," with no delinquency greater than 30 days, differed considerably as did the proportion with serious delinquencies (60 days or greater) and that approximately half of consumers with medical-only collections tradelines had otherwise clean credit reports. (Figures 12-14 below depict these differences).

FIGURE 12: INCIDENCE OF WORST NON COLLECTIONS DELINQUENCY APPEARING ON CREDIT RECORDS OF CONSUMERS WITH ONLY NON-MEDICAL COLLECTIONS TRADELINES (PERCENT OF RECORDS)

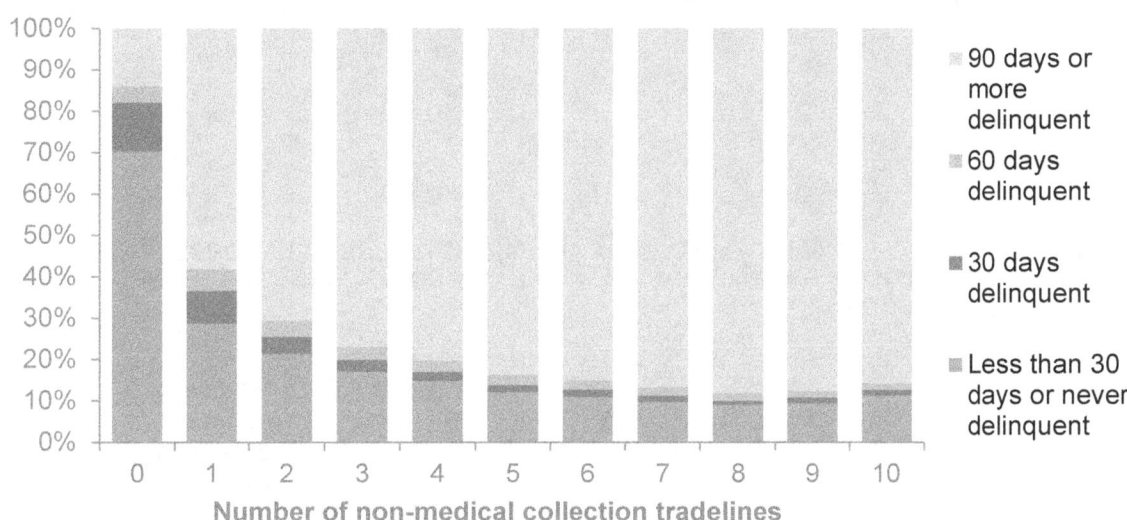

percent. This finding compared with 54 percent of consumers with only one medical collections tradeline. At two collections tradelines, the proportion of consumers with non-medical debt who had "clean" records dropped to 25 percent, while the proportion of "clean" records among consumers with two medical debt tradelines was 49 percent and for consumers with one of each type of collections tradeline, 34 percent.

WORST NON-COLLECTIONS DELINQUENCY APPEARING ON CREDIT RECORDS OF CONSUMERS WITH ONLY MEDICAL COLLECTIONS TRADELINES (PERCENT OF RECORDS)

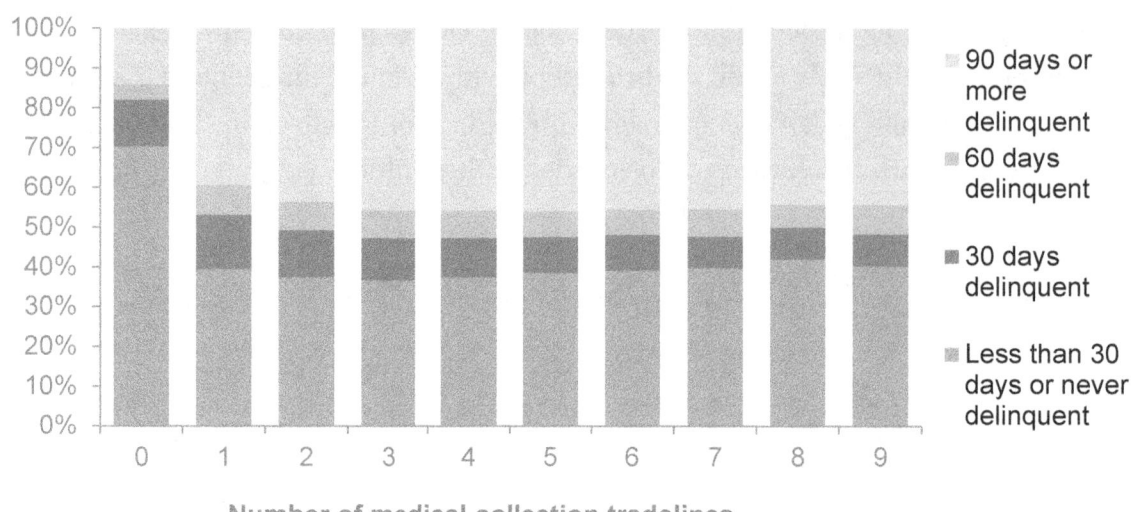

Number of medical collection tradelines

FIGURE 14: WORST NON-COLLECTIONS DELINQUENCY APPEARING ON CREDIT RECORDS OF CONSUMERS WITH BOTH MEDICAL AND NON-MEDICAL COLLECTIONS TRADELINES (PERCENT OF RECORDS)

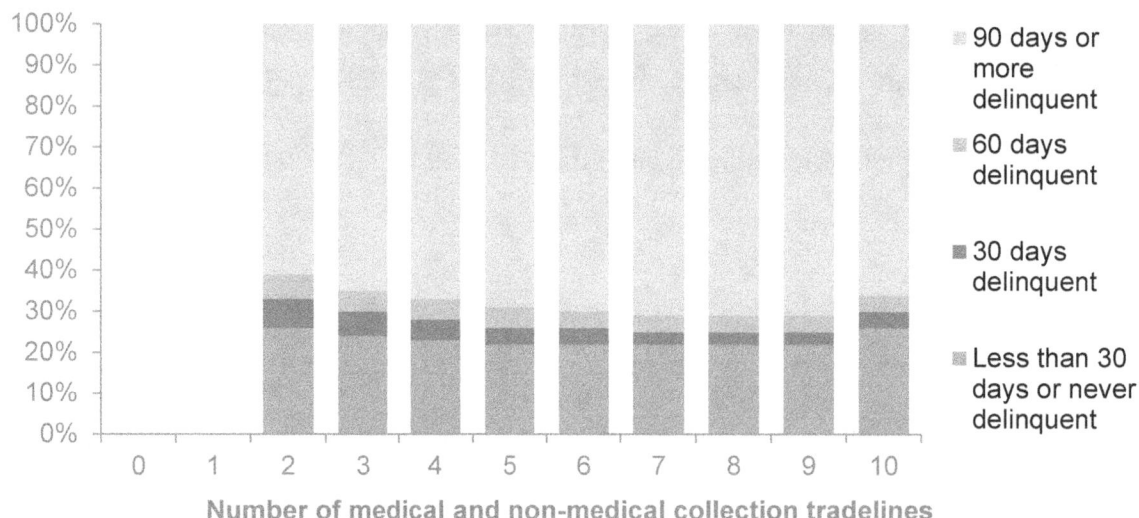

Number of medical and non-medical collection tradelines

These differences appear consistent out to 10 or more collections tradelines. Among consumers with 10 or more exclusively non-medical collections tradelines, only 13 percent of consumers had "clean" records, while 52 percent of consumers with 10 or more exclusively medical collections tradelines had 'clean' records. The higher the number of non-medical collections tradelines on their records, the lower the likelihood a consumer would have "clean" records. This was not the case for consumers with only medical collections. The percentage of consumers with 10 or more medical tradelines who had clean records was nearly the same as that among consumers with just one medical tradeline.

Consumers who have only medical debt in collections owe less debt in collections in total than consumers with only non-medical collections tradelines or both types of collections tradelines. Consumers with only medical collections tradelines have an average total unpaid amount owed (summing up all of their collections tradelines) of $1,766 ($438 median), while consumers with only non-medical collections owed a total of $4,098 on average ($1,042 median), and consumers with a combination of both types owed a total of $5,638 on average ($2,450 median). Figure 15 depicts the differences in the distribution of consumers in each group by total amounts reported as owed in collections tradelines.

FIGURE 15: DISTRIBUTION OF CONSUMERS BY AMOUNT OF UNPAID COLLECTIONS OWED AND COLLECTIONS TYPE

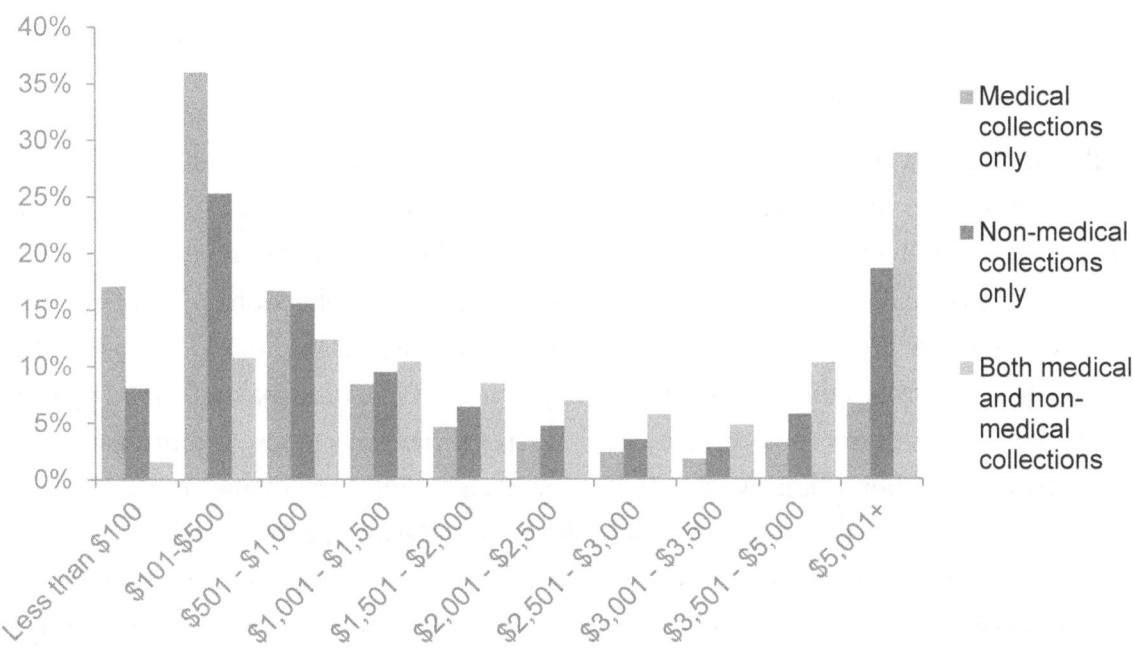

In summary, consumers who have only medical debt in collections differ in important ways from those who have other types of non-medical collections tradelines or both types on their records. Many more consumers with only medical collections demonstrate a tendency to pay their bills on time (have less than a 30 day delinquency) regardless of the number of collections tradelines, as compared to consumers in the other two groups. Additionally, given the smaller size of medical collections debt, consumers with exclusively medical collections tradelines owe smaller amounts on their debts in collection when compared to consumers in the other groups. More consumers in this group would presumably have a higher capacity to repay these debts from personal funds or available credit lines. The fact that consumers in this group have not repaid these debts, and yet otherwise indicate an ability and willingness to meet their obligations, suggests there is something different about these consumers' understanding of their debts and their reasons for not paying them.

4.4 Variability in medical collections tradeline incidence

In Section 3 of this paper we describe considerable variation across and within industries in collector furnishing practices. These include the decision to report a collections tradeline to the NCRAs and the timing of when the debt is considered sufficiently delinquent to be considered a collections account. The variability can be particularly high among medical providers and their collectors.

In a nationally fragmented health care market, prevailing local customs and practices and policies of the hospitals serving a particular area can affect the collections and furnishing practices of medical providers and their debt collectors. In addition, furnishing practices can be influenced by state and local laws and regulations that pertain to the collections practices and strategies those healthcare providers and collectors can employ. For example, In Colorado, when an insured consumer receives a bill from a healthcare provider that is only partially paid by the insurer, the provider must notify the person by mail at least thirty days before initiating any collection activity on the amount it is owed.[70] In California, a hospital or assignee of a hospital (including a collection agency working on behalf of the hospital) cannot report consumer nonpayment to a NCRA prior to 150 days after the initial billing date if the consumer is uninsured or if the consumer has an income that falls below 350 percent of the federal poverty level.[71,72]

---

[70] C.R.S. 6-20-202

[71] California Health and Safety Code §127425(d).

The incidence of both non-medical and medical collections tradelines on credit reports can vary widely by state, county, city and provider.[73] The incidence of non-medical collections tradelines ranges from 15 percent of consumer credit reports in the state with the lowest incidence to 34 percent in the state with the highest incidence. The incidence of medical collections tradelines varies considerably more by state, ranging from a low of 4 percent of consumers in the state with the lowest incidence to a high of 32 percent in the state with the highest incidence. While the incidence of medical collections in a state appears to be strongly correlated with the incidence of non-medical collections, some states' incidence of medical collections falls considerably below the level that might be expected given the incidence of non-medical collections; in other states reported medical debts are higher than one would expect.

4.5 Proposed new timing standards

Variations in the timing of when overdue medical accounts are sent for collections and when medical collections tradelines appear on credit reports may be affected by new rules for non-profit hospitals proposed by the Internal Revenue Service (IRS) under the Affordable Care Act (ACA).[74] If finalized as proposed, the IRS rules would require that before a non-profit hospital

---

[72] California Health and Safety Code refer to consumers with "high medical costs" as those with family incomes below 350 percent of the federal poverty level. For more information, see California Health and Safety Code §127400(g).

[73] Other important factors may also affect regional or state-by-state variations in medical debt incidence. These could include prevailing economic and demographic conditions (such as employment rates, average income, age distributions, and poverty rates). Such conditions would affect the number of consumers in a market who experience financial distress and who would likely be subject to debt collection on any type of delinquent account. Local conditions that would likely affect the incidence of medical collections tradelines above and beyond these economic and demographic factors could include characteristics of the local healthcare market (insurer or provider competition, prevalence of non-profit compared to for-profit hospitals, etc.) and state healthcare and social safety net policy (such as the availability of subsidized insurance coverage, support for low-cost primary care, Medicaid eligibility, charity care and reimbursement programs, etc.).

[74] Internal Revenue Service, New Requirements for 501(C)(3) Hospitals Under the Affordable Care Act (2014), *available at* http://www.irs.gov/Charities-&-Non-Profits/Charitable-Organizations/New-Requirements-for-501(c)(3)-Hospitals-Under-the-Affordable-Care-Act. Specifically, the proposed rules would require a non-profit hospital to:
  - establish written financial assistance and emergency medical care policies;

can begin collecting on bills, the consumer must be informed of the bills and the hospital's charitable care policies, and be given time to apply to determine their eligibility under these policies.

The proposed rules set a minimum period of 120 days following a hospital's billing date before it could engage in "extraordinary collection measures." Such measures explicitly include referring consumer bills to collection by a third-party agency collecting on a contingency basis and reporting the consumer's debt to a consumer reporting agency. Standardizing the debt aging period to 120 days from the billing date for medical collections would introduce new consistency regarding the age of these items and establish a floor for the severity of delinquency that they represent when they first appear on credit reports. Implementing a minimum age of delinquency threshold for reporting can also reduce the overall number of medical collections accounts that are reported by eliminating tradelines that may currently be reported early in the collections cycle (*i.e.* earlier than 120 days past due). In addition, mandating patient communications can improve consumers' awareness of the existence of their debts prior to the debt being referred to collection agencies or their appearance as medical collections tradelines on the consumers' credit reports.

The HFMA, an association of healthcare finance professionals, and the Association of Credit and Collection Professionals (ACA International, a trade association of collections professionals) released a draft list of best practices for patient billing, collections, and credit reporting last year that include similar provisions to the IRS's proposal with respect to the timing of credit reporting.[75]

- limit amounts charged for emergency or other medically necessary care to individuals eligible for assistance under the hospital's financial assistance policy;

- make reasonable efforts to determine whether an individual is eligible for assistance under the hospital's financial assistance policy before engaging in extraordinary collection actions against the individual; and

- conduct a community health needs assessment and adopt an implementation strategy at least once every three years.

[75] Medical Account Resolution Best Practices Issued, HFMA January 15, 2014.[Is there a link for this?]

5. Implications and conclusions

Our analysis of collections tradelines on consumer credit reports suggests that the system of collecting on consumers' debts and reporting collections tradelines introduces multiple points in which error can creep into the system. Significant questions exist as to the accuracy of collections tradeline reporting.

Furthermore, our analysis suggests that the presence of collections tradelines, even if accurately reported, can represent a wide range of consumer circumstances. The timing of their appearance can be dependent on the type of debt the consumer owes and the debt recovery strategies employed by creditors and their debt collectors. Given that nearly one third of all consumers have such items on their credit reports, a nuanced understanding of the circumstances that have given rise to the debts, how and when they are reported, and by whom they have been reported can be helpful in determining how best to use this information in assessing a consumer's creditworthiness.

Medical collections tradelines, which comprise over half of all collections tradelines and are found on nearly one in five consumers' credit reports, raise particular concerns. Both the complexity and confusion that accompanies the medical billing process and the variety of financial conditions of the consumers who incur medical debts indicate that the appearance of a medical collections tradeline on a credit report can reflect uniquely diverse financial circumstances and behavior among consumers with medical collections tradelines. The timing of when these tradelines appear on and disappear from consumers' credit reports is also influenced by factors that do not necessarily reflect on the consumer's behavior. Such factors include the time required for the claims adjudication process between provider and insurer, and the medical provider's policies and strategies regarding their use of collectors and the stage of delinquency at which they engage debt collectors to recover unpaid bills.

In light of these factors, the finding of the Bureau's May 2014 Data Point that the presence of medical collections tradelines on a consumer's credit report are less predictive of future delinquency on payments than non-medical collections is not surprising. Credit scoring models which differentiate medical collections from other collections are likely to more accurately reflect the actual creditworthiness of consumers.

Leading credit score developers report that until recent years, their models have treated the presence of collections tradelines as a one-dimensional attribute and have weighted the presence of collections tradelines the same, regardless of type of debt, amount owed, or unpaid versus paid status. As a result, credit scores can have underestimated the creditworthiness (overestimated the credit risk) of some consumers with certain accounts in collections, while overestimating the creditworthiness of other consumers with other collections tradelines.

Recent versions of widely used scoring models have begun differentiating between collections tradelines. One widely-used model introduced in 2008 (FICO 8) omits from consideration any collections tradeline below $100. Two recently-introduced models, VantageScore 3.0 from VantageScore and Fair,Isaac's FICO 9 both differentiate unpaid from paid collections in weighting collections tradelines. Earlier this year, FICO announced that its FICO 9 model would weight medical collections tradelines differently from non-medical collections tradelines and would remove paid collections tradelines. The developers report that they have incorporated these approaches to collections tradeline information in their new models to produce credit scores that are more predictive of a consumer's future credit behavior.

At the same time, rules (such as those proposed at the federal level for non-profit hospitals) or industry best practices (as drafted by ACA International and HFMA) that standardize when delinquent medical accounts can be reported as collections tradelines could introduce more consistency in the information about medical collections furnished to the NCRAs. Such rules and practices could support greater predictability of future credit behavior through scoring models.

The Bureau will continue its efforts to assess the accuracy of information reported to and contained on credit reports and to identify steps that various stakeholders can take to improve the accuracy, integrity, and consistency of data in the system, consumers' awareness of how the system works, and consumers' ability to make sure their credit reports accurately represent their credit histories.

APPENDIX A:

Consumer medical collections complaints

Table 3 summarizes the principal reason categories for collections complaints that we have been able to identify as being about medical accounts and complaints about other types of collection accounts.

TABLE 3: PRIMARY REASON GIVEN FOR COMPLAINTS TO CFPB OFFICE OF CONSUMER RESPONSE REGARDING COLLECTIONS (SHARE OF REASONS GIVEN FOR MEDICAL AND ALL OTHER COLLECTIONS)

Most Frequently Stated Reason for Complaint	Collections Complaints Identified as Medical	All Other Collections Complaints
Debt is not mine	23.0%	22.8%
Frequent or repeated calls	7.4%	11.3%
Not given enough information to verify debt	14.5%	9.00%
Debt was paid	20.0%	8.5%
Threatened arrest/ jail if do not pay	0.9%	8.5%
Threatened to take legal action	3.4%	6.7%
Attempted to collect wrong amount	7.6%	4.7%
Talked to a third party about my debt	2.9%	3.9%
Threatened to sue on too old debt	1.2%	3.3%
Impersonated an attorney or official	0.7%	3.0%
Right to dispute notice not received	5.1%	2.5%

www.ingramcontent.com/pod-product-compliance
Lightning Source LLC
Chambersburg PA
CBHW080611180526
45168CB00007B/2871